Ex-Library: Friends of
Lake County Public Library

W9-CAZ-318

Shenyang

NORTH KOREA

Sea of
Japan

Beijing

JAPAN

Tianjin

Luoyang

SOUTH KOREA

Kaifeng

North
Pacific
Ocean

A

Shanghai
Hangzhou

Yellow
Sea

Taibei

TAIWAN

Guangzhou

Hong Kong

Macau

South
China
Sea

Philippine
Sea

PHILIPPINES

Made in China
Ideas and Inventions from Ancient China

By Suzanne Williams

Selected illustrations by Andrea Fong

Pacific View Press
Berkeley, California

LAKE COUNTY PUBLIC LIBRARY

3 3113 01670 0710

To Michelle, Mara, and Luke

Acknowledgements

This book would not exist without the help of many, many people. My deepest gratitude for assistance in research, interviews, and illustrations to Mark Halperin, doctoral candidate, University of California, Berkeley; Hanni Forester and John Stucky, San Francisco Asian Art Museum; Mary Kay Ryan, Dipl. Ac.; Lixin Huang, American College of Traditional Chinese Medicine, San Francisco; Dr. Martin Lee; Norm Sperling, Chabot Observatory; Evelyn Chiang; and David Lei, Chinese Performing Arts Foundation.

My thanks to my student readers, Tanner, Tara, Kyle, Shay, Laura, Brent, and their teacher Brooke Petersen, and to editors Pam Zumwalt and Nancy Ippolito for patient support as we made this book, illustrator Andrea Fong and designer Mark Ong.

And to my family for listening and listening.

Credits

Andrea Fong: cover, pages 4–5, 7, 11, 13, 23, 25, 35, 38, 46–47

Kenneth DeWoskin: Zhou Bells page 9

Science & Society Picture Library, London: Seismograph, page 25

Metropolitan Museum of Art, Gift of the Dillon Fund, 1973 (1973.120.3): page 12

National Geographic Society: pages 14–15

Ontario Science Centre: pages 16 and 37

Asian Art Museum of San Francisco, The Avery Brundage Collection: Pages 26, 42–43

The British Library, London: page 28

Topkapi Museum, Istanbul: page 36

Sterling Publishing Company., Inc., New York, from *The Mongol Warlords* by David Nicolle, ©1990 by Firebird Books Ltd., Text ©1990 by David Nicolle: page 45

Cover illustration:
Carpenters, bricklayers, blacksmiths, calligraphers, and others demonstrate their skills

Copyright ©1996 by Suzanne Williams
Cover and text design by Mark Ong
Selected illustrations by Andrea Fong

All rights reserved. No part of this book may be used or reproduced in any manner whatsoever without permission in writing from the publisher. Address inquiries to Pacific View Press, P.O. Box 2657, Berkeley, CA 94702.

Library of Congress Catalog Card Number: 96-69368
ISBN 1-881896-14-5

Printed in China by Twin Age Ltd

Table of Contents

-1600	-1400	-1200	-1000	-800	-600	-400	-200	0	200	400	600	800	1000	1200	1400	1600	1800	1949

Xia Dynasty

Shang Dynasty (North China)

Zhou Dynasty (North China)

Warring States Period

Qin Dynasty

Han Dynasty

Three Kingdoms

Northern and Southern Dynasties

Sui Dynasty

Tang Dynasty

Five Dynasties

Song Dynasty

Liao (Qidan)

Jin (Ruzhen)

Yuan (Mongol) Dynasty

Ming Dynasty

Qing (Manchu) Dynasty

Republic of China

Peoples Republic of China

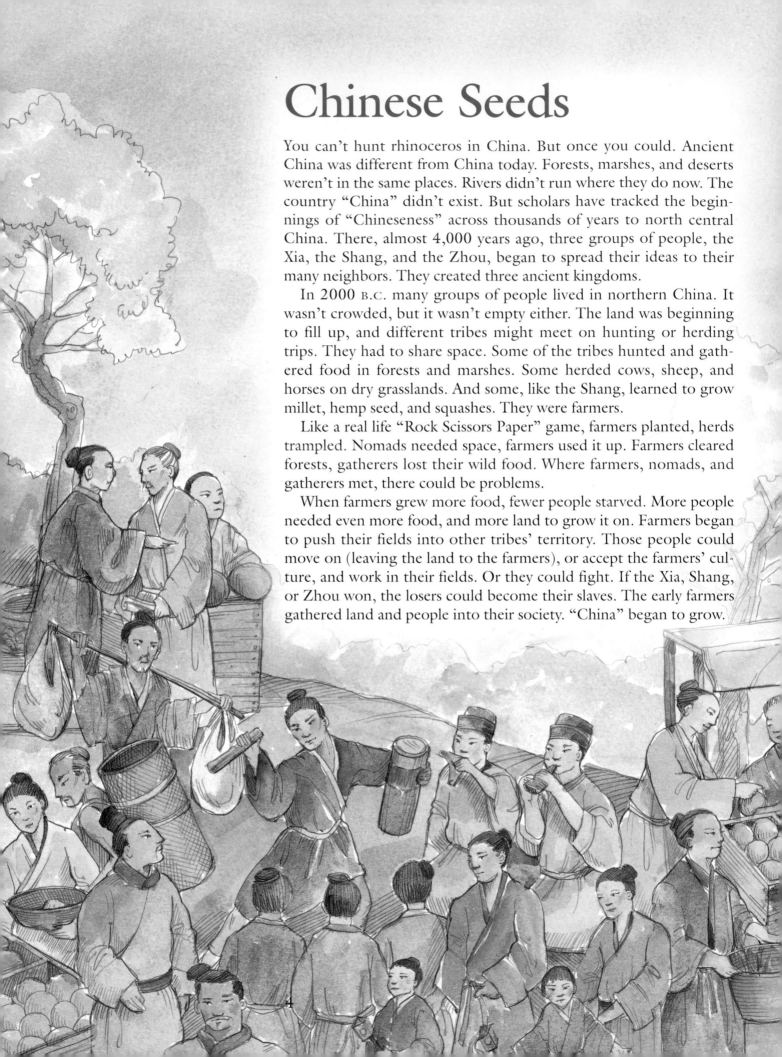

Chinese Seeds

You can't hunt rhinoceros in China. But once you could. Ancient China was different from China today. Forests, marshes, and deserts weren't in the same places. Rivers didn't run where they do now. The country "China" didn't exist. But scholars have tracked the beginnings of "Chineseness" across thousands of years to north central China. There, almost 4,000 years ago, three groups of people, the Xia, the Shang, and the Zhou, began to spread their ideas to their many neighbors. They created three ancient kingdoms.

In 2000 B.C. many groups of people lived in northern China. It wasn't crowded, but it wasn't empty either. The land was beginning to fill up, and different tribes might meet on hunting or herding trips. They had to share space. Some of the tribes hunted and gathered food in forests and marshes. Some herded cows, sheep, and horses on dry grasslands. And some, like the Shang, learned to grow millet, hemp seed, and squashes. They were farmers.

Like a real life "Rock Scissors Paper" game, farmers planted, herds trampled. Nomads needed space, farmers used it up. Farmers cleared forests, gatherers lost their wild food. Where farmers, nomads, and gatherers met, there could be problems.

When farmers grew more food, fewer people starved. More people needed even more food, and more land to grow it on. Farmers began to push their fields into other tribes' territory. Those people could move on (leaving the land to the farmers), or accept the farmers' culture, and work in their fields. Or they could fight. If the Xia, Shang, or Zhou won, the losers could become their slaves. The early farmers gathered land and people into their society. "China" began to grow.

Living Chinese

In ancient China you might live in a pit . . . or a palace. High-class Xia and Shang people lived in big houses made of earth, timbers, and thatched roofs. In the same village, working people had small pit houses dug into the ground. Because the Xia people lived so long ago, scholars are still piecing together their picture of Xia life from legends, ancient books, and the remains of villages.

We know more about the next dynasty (a government like a kingdom), the Shang. The Xia and the Shang were separate tribes but they may have shared some land and ideas. First the Xia were more powerful and then the Shang grew stronger. Between 1700 and 1100 B.C. the Shang had 30 kings and ruled many tribes, including the Xia. Shang upper-class people ruled and chose kings. These people supervised workers, led battles, and were rich. The lower-class people might be farmers, builders, potters, or metal workers. There were slaves captured in battles or sentenced to slavery for crimes. Some people ended up as human sacrifices in Shang graves.

The king made all the important decisions about the people. He decided when they should clear more fields, move the capital city, or go to war. The king used information from shamans, or priests, who guessed at the future, to help him decide. Once the king made up his mind, he convinced the people his idea was right. The Shang believed the king's ancestors lived in heaven and spoke to him through shamans. The ancestors had ideas about what the people should do. If the people made those heavenly relatives angry, terrible things, such as earthquakes, floods, and bad hunting trips could happen. If the king and his ancestors couldn't convince people to do what he said, he could threaten to punish or kill them. The king and the upper-class people were powerful. They got things done.

Four thousand years ago, the Xia and the Shang began to do things Chinese people still do. Shang people made silk, pottery, and beautiful metal work in bronze. They had a system of writing, a powerful government, and shamans who predicted the future. Shang farmers grew enough food to feed the upper-class people and the artists, soldiers, and priests. Chinese culture, "Chineseness," was beginning.

The Shang people saw life and death as a single event. They believed dead people changed forms but continued to live the same kind of life close to home. The dead needed food, furniture, clothes, and games for that invisible life. They might need servants or companions and animals to be sacrificed and buried with them. When a person died, families gathered supplies for the "move" to the invisible world and buried them with the body. Children needed toys, musicians needed instruments, and rich people needed their wealth. Shang people made what they needed for every day living, and then they had to make more things to send with the dead to the invisible world.

5

Bronze

Pretend you're living in ancient times. Maybe you put some rocks in your cooking fire to hold up some meat. While the fire blazes, you notice something shiny running out of the rocks. It's so hot you can't touch it. The next morning, when you go to the fire pit, the stuff is cold and hard. You heat it up again and it runs. Now you try digging a hole for it to run into. When it cools it holds its shape. You could have just discovered how to cast metal!

Shang people cast bronze . . . a mixture of copper and tin. Bronze was the first metal ancient people learned to use. The Shang people made spear and arrow heads, knife blades, tools, and cooking pots. They made fancy pots and drinking vessels for religious and government ceremonies. Today Shang bronzes are beautiful reminders of their culture. Thousands of years ago, good bronze weapons may have helped the Shang win battles.

It took a lot of work to cast bronze. Metal ore had to be mined and hauled to the workshop . . . often in capital cities or near rich households. The ore was heated in earth or brick furnaces to melt the metal. The hot metal ran out of the rocks, ready for casting.

Workers carried hot liquid bronze quickly to fill the molds. The bronze was heavy and the pots could be big. All the metal had to be poured in a short time. Some vessels may have needed hundreds of workers to cast them.

The Chinese recycled old bronze tools by melting and recasting them. Vessels and pots were saved and often buried in tombs.

The Chinese found ways to separate the metals in rocks. Rocks with lead and copper could be heated in one furnace. The lead melted first and came out through a hole low on the furnace. Copper melted second and came out through a higher hole.

When workers cast huge bells or pots they had to use metal from several furnaces. Sometimes, the mold for the pot was put into a hole lower than the furnaces. Metal workers dug ditches from the furnaces to the mold. Then they could let the metal run out of the furnace and into the mold, like water down the gutter into the drain.

Artists made two clay molds, a center mold and an outer mold, to shape the hot, liquid bronze. The bronze would be poured between the molds like filling for a sandwich. They made the center mold the size and shape of the pot they wanted. Next they put sections of soft clay over the center mold, forming them to its shape. These became the outer mold.

Designs, words, and decorations had to be carved on the INSIDE of the outer mold sections (the INSIDE of the mold shaped the OUTSIDE of the bronze). They carved the designs backwards, like mirror writing, so they would turn out right on the finished piece.

To make room for the bronze between the molds, they trimmed some clay from the center mold. Last, they fitted the outer mold sections around the center mold, sealing them together with mud. They poured in liquid bronze. After the bronze hardened, they removed the outside molds and broke the center mold to get it out of the pot.

Legend says that King Yu, first king of the Xia dynasty, had superhuman powers. He cast the first bronze vessels. He made nine, one for each of his provinces. He had the rules of his kingdom and information about irrigation written on the vessels and cast them in bronze so they would last a long time. King Yu also directed the water into China's rivers after a great flood had covered the earth, deciding where each should run.

LOST WAX

Where does wax go when it gets hot? It melts. That is what happened to the "lost wax" molds that metal workers used in later centuries. They covered the center mold with thick wax. They could carve the wax to look exactly as their finished piece would look. They covered the wax model with a thin layer of clay. When the clay hardened, workers poured hot bronze between the two layers of clay. The wax melted and the mold was lost. Lost wax pieces were one of a kind!

The Chinese gift for casting bronze allowed them to build large, precise, and beautiful instruments like the seismograph and armillary sphere.

The Chinese used 12 musical tones to measure length and weight. They measured length by plucking 12 special strings. Long strings play lower notes than short ones do. The 12 notes matched 12 different lengths of string. Those lengths could be used to measure many things. Weight was measured by the weight of millet grains that fit into specially tuned pitch pipes. Low pitched pipes held more grain, high pitched ones held less.

Shang and Zhou

While the Shang were busy ruling, the group that would finally destroy their royal family was growing. West of the Shang lands, the Zhou herded animals and cleared farm land. They probably didn't worry the Shang one bit. The Zhou had their own land and their own kings.

But as Shang territory grew, the Zhou met them more and more. Finally, the Zhou were included in the Shang kingdom. Zhou paid tribute (honorary gifts and taxes) to the Shang king. A Zhou leader, Ji Li, led battles for the Shang. He won, but the Shang executed him. Later on, the Shang king, Wu Yi, died in Zhou territory. The two kingdoms were becoming enemies.

The Zhou didn't have as many people as the Shang, but the Shang had other enemies. When the Shang began to battle their eastern neighbors, the Zhou took their opportunity. They organized an army of their own people and of other angry tribes. Together they invaded the Shang capital and won the battle in only one day. The Shang king, seeing he had lost his city, killed himself by jumping into a fire.

The Zhou conquered the Shang, but now they had to rule them. There weren't a lot of Zhou people. They needed the support of the Shang. According to Zhou records, the Shang king was greedy, ignored his people, drank too much, and gave out grisly punishments. The Shang should be glad to be rid of him. Heaven itself took power away from the cruel Shang and gave it to the honorable Zhou. The Zhou said this to convince the Shang people to accept them. It became a Chinese tradition to overthrow a wicked ruler to replace him with a moral one.

The Zhou king took over, but he didn't change the government or the people's ways. He used Shang officials in his government, and when he decided to settle new territory he sent a mix of Shang and Zhou people to do the job. At the new settlement, they were ordered to include the native people in their group.

The Zhou ruled by including people. The king was number one. Below him were dukes and earls who had their own groups of people and territory. The Zhou accepted different cultures. They used their favorite parts of Shang culture themselves.

The Zhou continued to create bronze vessels and bells. They cast them for important occasions such as winning a battle, or a visit from the king. Often, they wrote the history of the event in the bronze . . . like writing today on plaques or statues describing historic occasions. Because they were cast in bronze and often were buried in storage rooms or in tombs, these records are still readable. They are a treasure of information. Zhou bronze technology made history.

Bells

There were no CDs or radios in ancient China. There weren't any tapes. Zhou people made their own music. In an orchestra of bone chimes, stringed instruments, and flutes, the most majestic instrument was the bronze bells. Sounds boomed and trembled from big bells, or rang high and clear from small ones. These bells came from the same bronze workshops that cast vessels and tools.

Zhou bells didn't have clappers inside. A musician struck them to make them play. Each bell was tuned to ring two different pitches, one if the bell was hit high, and another if it was hit near the bottom. Whole sets of bells were tuned to match each other's tones. Noblemen tuned their bells to match the king's bells.

Matching these bells in a bronze workshop was not a simple job. It sometimes took hundreds of workers to cast one piece. Imagine how careful the designer had to be to make bells that matched in size and tone.

The bells were used for ceremonies and for music. But they might have had another use. Since they didn't have clappers, they may have started out as grain scoops. The king didn't ask for gold or money when he collected taxes, but grain. He wanted to know he was getting the right amount. Matched sets of bells could be used to measure exact amounts of grain for the king.

Music traveled across valleys and through towns. It made sense, to the Zhou, that sound could travel to the invisible world of the dead, or to the heavens or into the earth. The bronze Zhou bells were important to religious and government ceremonies. They sent messages.

The man who owned the bells gained respect. He had to be rich enough to have them made, and important enough to be listened to.

It takes lots of work to grow rice. It must be planted in fertilized fields. Rice seeds need to sprout before they are planted. They are planted in a flooded field, allowed to grow bigger, then transplanted into larger fields.

The fields need to be irrigated and weeded many times. In early China, farmers combed bugs off plants with a bamboo comb or coated the plants with special oil to kill insects.

Last, farmers drain the fields, cut the rice, separate the kernels of rice from the stalks, and store it.

JING FIELDS
The Zhou divided their fields into groups of nine. The arrangement looked a lot like the character, *jing*, 井 or well. They are called well fields. Eight of the fields were planted by eight farmers. The farmers worked the ninth field together, giving the harvest from that field to their lord.

Agriculture

Feeding the People

Generation after generation, Chinese people have farmed. They farmed in Shang times and they farm now. Farming was thought to be the best job. No wonder. Farmers supported everyone! They raised millet, beans, and rice. The Shang people probably traded for wheat (which first grew in the Middle East and Central Asia). Later Chinese grew it, especially in North China.

When the crops were good people didn't starve, but more people needed more food. The food could come from new farms or it could come from working harder, and working smarter.

One way to farm smarter was to bring water to dry land . . . to irrigate. Emperors built canals and dams. Irrigated land produced more food. But it took hard work to keep the system running. Even when a river flowed right by a farm, the water had to be moved into the fields. The Chinese invented the chain pump to do that.

The chain pump, invented by 100 B.C., uses square paddles connected together like a chain. The paddle chain moves from under water, into a trough, through the trough to the level of the field. Here, the trough stops and the water falls into the irrigation ditch. The farmer could move the paddles in different ways. He could turn a wheel by walking. Imagine turning a bicycle gear and moving the chain. Later, power came from oxen, water wheels, or even wind. Using the chain pump, farmers could quickly raise water about 15 feet from rivers or irrigation ditches into their fields.

Irrigation helped grow rice. Rice grows best in clean water. As Chinese people moved south looking for new land to farm, rice farming became more important. South China had more water for better irrigating. The water didn't come from big muddy rivers, but from springs and small rivers in the hills. Rice grew well in this new area. And when a rice farmer worked harder, he got more rice. When more people needed to be fed, rice farmers could work harder weeding, transplanting, and caring for their crop. More work gave them more food.

Think about how much easier it would be to dig up a field with a plow instead of with a stick. Early farmers used wooden plows. But the tip (plowshare) would often break. The Chinese discovered how to cast, or pour, iron into molds. After the Zhou dynasty they began to make iron plowshares. By the Han dynasty, there were workshops all over China making plenty of pots, swords, and plowshares. Now imagine you are a farmer who owns a plowshare that doesn't break! You'd be glad to have that sturdy tool.

10

Even better, Chinese plows had a special piece called a "mold-board." Moldboards fit onto the plowshare and pushed the plowed dirt to the side, away from the row, turning it upside down. A plow with a moldboard worked something like a steam iron pushing through dirt. The dirt would be broken by the tip of the "iron" and moved away by the broader part behind. If the plow had a mold-board, the dirt didn't pile up in front of the plow or muck up the plowshare. Plows with moldboards were a great labor saving invention!

LEGEND OF HOU JI

Hou Ji is honored as one of the earliest farmers. Here is his story: Abandoned as a baby, Hou Ji was left with cows and sheep. People tried many times to get rid of the boy, but the animals rescued him. Finally the people took him back. He grew up to be an excellent farmer. He made all kinds of grains and farm tools. King Yao (one of the earliest kings in Chinese legends) asked Hou Ji to teach the people how to farm. He gave people a special stone called the Five Crop Stone that produced food.

11

Nomads and Farmers

Opposing Forces

There were lots of different nomad tribes living to the north and west of the Chinese. Different tribes were powerful at different times. The nomads were good horse soldiers. After all, they worked on horseback. Nomads probably invented the stirrup. By the year 300, the Chinese were making stirrups from bronze and iron. Using stirrups, a rider could balance better, stand while riding, or lean farther across his horse. Stirrups gave nomads and Chinese an advantage in riding and in fighting.

The wind blows off the Gobi desert across miles and miles of dry grassland north of China. The land wasn't much good for farming. It was good for grazing animals. Nomads drove their herds from place to place, changing grazing areas when they needed. To the south, Chinese people were farmers. Sometimes the people who lived where grasslands and farms met traded with each other and married each other. More often they had problems. Farmers didn't want animals tramping their fields. From the earliest times, nomads and Chinese fought over land.

To make things worse, farmers sometimes had food when nomads had none. The Chinese also made beautiful things like silk that the nomads wanted. If they couldn't buy these things from the Chinese, sometimes nomads rode in and took them. The Great Wall of China was built to keep nomads away from Chinese farmers, but it could not stop wars. Wars and bad feelings between nomads and Chinese continued from ancient times into this century.

Chinese farmers often used oxen to work in fields. The oxen had big shoulders. Farmers put a yolk in front of the ox's shoulders and the ox pulled against it. It was more difficult to use horses for field work. Horses' shoulders slope, and a yolk would pull right off. Harnesses with straps across the horse's neck choked him, giving him trouble breathing and working.

By 100 B.C., the Chinese invented the horse collar. It allowed the horse to pull across his chest and shoulders to move a heavy load the way oxen do. Chinese soldiers used horses with collars to pull their chariots. Farmers used them to plow fields and to pull carts.

Crossbow

First Class Weapon

The crossbow was the assault weapon of the ancient world. The Chinese guarded it as a top-level military secret. In 200 B.C. there was a law against taking a crossbow out of China. This was not a weapon to allow enemies to copy. But legend says the crossbow was invented to make peace, to calm the fighting that broke out at the end of the Zhou dynasty. A man named Qin from Chu made it to control warring feudal lords.

The lords the Zhou kings had created were getting more and more powerful and the king less. The king began to have rivals. By 700 B.C. the Zhou king, although still called the ruler, was more like one of many nobles, ruling the small territory around his capitol at Luoyang. The other lords had their territories too. Some were more powerful than the king. What followed was years of fighting between the lords of the many small states that had been created by the Zhou kings. Historians named this time the "Warring States Period."

War changed. The lords called up thousands of men to fight on foot. Some states had armies of at least 100,000. These new armies had new weapons. Bronze swords were cast with extra tin to make them extra sharp. Halberds, a combination of spear and battle ax, had blades that could cut a hair. And, by 400 or 500 B.C., men were armed with crossbows.

Crossbows could be pulled tighter and aimed better than regular bows. Some crossbows were so big they needed a team of men to load the arrow and pull the bowstring. These weapons shot farther and harder than normal bow and arrows. A crossbow arrow could pierce armor.

The key to a crossbow was its trigger. The trigger let the archer use his whole body to pull the bow string, often standing on the bow and pulling the string with both hands. He hooked the string behind two hooks, held in place by the trigger. The hooks held the string while the archer aimed his bow. He released the bowstring and arrow by pulling the trigger, like a gun. Over 2,000 years ago, Chinese government workshops made thousands of mass-produced triggers.

Things aren't always what we expect. Crossbows were also used to shoot cables across canyons as a first step in building suspension or hanging bridges. Kites were sometimes used to drop bombs of gunpowder into walled cities.

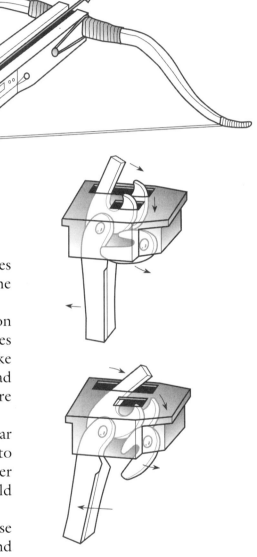

Crossbow triggers were made from four pieces of metal held together with two bolts. They fit together like a strong puzzle . . . until someone pulled the trigger. The trigger held a support piece in place. When the archer pulled the trigger, the support fell down, allowing the weight and hooks to fall, releasing the bow string.

Qin

One Empire, One Way

Thousands of soldiers met in battle after battle. Finally, only seven large Chinese states remained. It would take a strong man, a strong army, and plenty of supplies to win them all. King Ying Zheng of the state of Qin had the winning combination. He called up men from the fields to fight, armed them with the best weapons, and fed them from fields irrigated by new canals. Technology gave his army an edge.

King Zheng's troops beat the other states one after the other: Han, Zhao, Wei, Chu, Yan, and Qi. In seven years the Qin kingdom won China. In 221 B.C., King Zheng proclaimed himself the Emperor. He took a new name, Shihuangdi, The First Great Emperor. He was 38.

The new emperor ruled with strict laws. Punishments were harsh. Someone who littered could be whipped. He rewarded people who helped him, but not with land. He was in charge of all the land. He allowed peasants to own land and to move if they wished. He moved noblemen to his capital city. As he conquered other states, he built an exact copy of each king's palace in his capitol city. Emperor Qin collected the weapons from people in conquered states and melted them down. He had them cast into bells and statues.

L ike the Qin kings before him who built great canals and roads, Qin Shihuangdi built over 4,000 miles of roads. His most famous project began in 214 B.C.—the original Great Wall of China. A military project meant to protect Chinese from nomads of the northwest, Qin's wall was lengthened, improved and rebuilt by emperors over the next 1,800 years.

Emperor Qin ordered people all over China to use the same weights and lengths to measure things. Cart axles had to be the same width so all carts could travel in the same ruts in the roads. He ordered everyone in his empire to use the same types of coins. Scholars studied the characters used for writing in different parts of China and made one set that everyone had to use. This emperor could force people to do things the same way. That one way helped Chinese people to work together.

Find at Xi'an

Faces of the Past

Shihuangdi looked throughout his life for a potion that could make him live forever. In the meantime, he prepared his tomb at Mt. Li. He died at 49, while he was touring his eastern land. Two thousand years later, archeologists found his tomb at Mt. Li, near the modern city of Xi'an. Since 1974, they have been digging up around his grave.

What archeologists found was over 7,000 life-sized statues . . . an army made from pottery. This is the largest ceramic project ever! Think of all the people who had to work together to make these figures. How much clay had to be dug and carried to the workshops? How many kilns had to be set up to fire them hard?

There are crossbow archers, foot soldiers, and cavalry. There are generals and their horses and chariots. In 1985 archeologists found stables with terra cotta stable boys, horses, and other animals. Shihuangdi's army shows us weapons and armor, harness and cart designs, and gives an idea of the Qin army's military planning.

Shihuangdi wanted these soldiers to accompany him to the next world. Instead they became messengers to us today.

The soldiers from Xi'an each have a different face. Their bodies were molded for easy production, but their faces are the faces of real people. They look almost alive. Looking at a soldier from Xi'an, you can see how he dressed and how he carried his weapon. You can see the hairs on his moustache and the way he tied his shoes.

15

Paper

Fabric of North and South

Think of all the things we do with paper. It's not just for books and writing. We use it for money, to wrap packages, and to make decorations. We use paper in the bathroom. So did the Chinese. The oldest piece of paper that still exists was found in a Chinese tomb built about 86 B.C. at the beginning of the Han dynasty. (Paper is different from papyrus. Papyrus, made from pounded plants, was invented by Egyptians.) How did the Chinese invent paper? No one knows for sure.

Han China was centered in the north part of today's China. People in north China would wash old rags or the waste from silk cocoons before they used them to stuff quilts. Maybe folks were washing rags and drained the water over a mat. The left-over threads and lint might have stuck to the mat the way hair and soap collect in a shower drain. That wet fuzz would dry into something like paper. That's one idea of how paper was invented.

Non-Chinese people lived in the south. They had their own ways, including pounding mulberry tree bark into large sheets. They pounded the bark until it was up to ten times its original size. They used it for clothes. Maybe the Chinese learned about using plant fibers from these southern neighbors. We know they made paper from many kinds of plants. The earliest papers were made from hemp (the marijuana plant). Later, paper makers used mulberry bark, bamboo, straw, and even seaweed to make paper.

The first paper wasn't used for writing. Writing was done on bamboo, wood, stone, bronze, and silk. Paper was thick and spongy. People used it like cloth. Chinese men had paper jackets and hats. There were paper shoes, blankets, and even paper armor, made from thick folded paper. It was light and didn't rust. But, keep it out of muddy fields!

Of course, Chinese people started using paper for books and for writing too. Once they began to make books from paper, Chinese scholars had to keep the paper from damage. Insects eat paper, and the sun can yellow it. There were recipes for adding chemicals to color paper and for killing insects that tried to eat it. Some Chinese books, with good care, have lasted hundreds of years.

Over the centuries, papermaking became an important craft. Chinese began big paper-making workshops. Special papers were made for important projects. Su Yi Jian (A.D. 957–995) described papermakers pouring one sheet of paper 50 feet long. It was so big they used the bottom of a boat to hold the wet pulp. In the 16th century,

The first books were made from bamboo that was rolled and tied. Writing on the bamboo strips went up and down, like the bamboo. Traditional Chinese writing went top to bottom.

northern Chinese people saved scraps of old paper to make into recycled, fine, white paper.

Today we use paper instead of papyrus or the parchment skins early Europeans used for writing. Why? We can make paper cheaply from all sorts of fibers. It's easy to make a lot at one time. It can be mass produced.

The Chinese explained the invention of paper like this: Cai Lun served in the imperial court in A.D. 75. He was in charge of making instruments and weapons. Ancient people wrote on silk or bamboo tablets. Since silk was expensive and bamboo heavy, Cai Lun had the idea to make paper. He presented his idea to the emperor and was praised. He became the Marquis Cai, and paper has been used since that time. He is honored as the God of Papermaking. His picture hangs in paper mills and paper shops in China and Japan.

At first, mourners buried real objects in graves for the dead to use in the invisible world. Gradually, they began to bury models of the real things. Han people put small clay objects in their tombs—animals, farm buildings, servants, or soldiers. Paper models finally replaced the real objects and pottery models in tombs. The Tang government (A.D. 618–906) made special "spirit money" to burn at funerals. This money was only good for ghosts. Tiny paper cars, furniture, and "spirit money" are still used by some Chinese mourners.

Papermakers boiled plants into a soupy pulp. They dipped a screen into the pulp and let it stiffen. When it was solid enough to lift off the screen, they hung the sheet of paper to dry.

17

Scientific Traditions

At holiday time we all have different traditions. French children put out a shoe for Père Noël to fill with candy. Jewish children spin a dreidel. Chinese children get bright red envelopes of New Year's money. We do things differently, but we all celebrate. Chinese scientists and inventors came from groups with different customs and ideas, but in the end, they all learned things that helped everyone.

The scientists lived in a world of Chinese traditions. Some scientists were Daoist priests who practiced folk medicine or spent their lives looking for a potion to make people live forever. Daoists were fine alchemists (early chemists). One of these priests may have been trying to imitate the cycles that he saw in nature with chemicals or looking for a long-life potion. Instead he invented gunpowder.

Other scientists were government officials (Confucians). For them, studying the stars or designing a new way to move barges up a river was a job. They served the empire, predicting comets or correcting the calendar to keep the emperor in harmony with nature and his people.

Many inventors were ordinary people who needed something. Women living in a war zone invented matches, making their lives a little easier. A printer invented moveable type. Horse-riding nomads invented stirrups.

Confucians and Daoists often seemed to be on different sides in government, religion, and science. Confucians were conservative and logical and served the government. Daoists were practical and magical and served the common people. In fact, Daoists served emperors in ceremonies and as doctors. Village leaders, who were Confucians, asked Daoists to get rid of ghosts and bad spirits. Confucians worked in the smallest villages, serving the most common people. Confucians and Daoists often worked together. Both added to each other's knowledge.

Confucius

YIN AND YANG

Since ancient times, Chinese people have classified things as yin or yang. Yin is female, dark, and cool. Yang is male, light, and warm. The world and the people and things in it are always changing. Yin and yang change too. They are labels for the relationship between two things. A boy might be yin to his older brother and yang to his baby sister. He's the same boy. The relationship changes. Chinese scientists used the idea of yin and yang to describe eclipses, prescribe medicines, and explain earthquakes.

18

Two Great Men

About 500–300 B.C., great thinkers from around the world began developing their ideas . . . Socrates and Aristotle in Greece, Buddha in India, and Confucius and Lao Zi in China. Both Lao Zi, the founder of Daoism, and Confucius grew up just before the Warring States period. It must have been a terrifying time. Kings were battling or tricking each other with spies and plots. Regular people suffered. Confucius liked the order he learned about in the old Zhou kings' government. He wanted to see peace and order in his time. We know less about Lao Zi, but he retreated to a simple life and also looked for order in nature and in his own heart.

They created two philosophies. Lao Zi emphasized knowing when "enough is enough." His followers looked for The Way through nature and accepting their lot in life. They collected folk knowledge and ancient traditions. Daoism became a people's religion.

Confucius taught that life was a chain of relationships between father and son, ruler and subject, teacher and student. If each did his part, the world would be calm and happy. Good men would be men of justice and morality. Rulers would be allowed to rule because they took care of their people. Officials of the government would be well educated, thoughtful men.

Confucianism and Daoism are practiced by millions of people today. Confucius' idea that people can improve themselves and society through education and Lao Zi's idea that people should be happy with the natural order of the world, balance each other. In China and East Asia people can accept both ideas. The same person may use both philosophies. She may be more Daoist at one age, more Confucist at another. She blends the ideas. They are like hot and cold, black and white, tall and short . . . opposites that go together. Each part helps you understand the other.

Lao Zi

FIVE PHASES
Nature is constantly changing. Daoists explained these changes with the five phases. The five phases have been used to describe many different things: life, the universe, diseases, dynasties. The phases can change in order, like a wheel turning, or they can balance each other, like kids on a seesaw.

Each phase has a color, a direction, a planet, and a season of the year that goes with it.

Wood: Green, spring, east, dawn, Jupiter

Fire: Red, summer, south, midday, Mars

Earth: Yellow, late summer, center, late afternoon

Metal: White, autumn, west, dusk, Venus

Water: Black, winter, north, midnight, Mercury

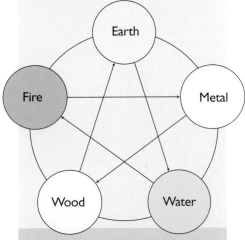

Qin Shihuangdi believed in the Daoist Five Phases. He thought his empire represented water. He took black for his color. This showed his dynasty as part of a cycle. The Yellow Emperor was from the earth. The Xia Dynasty was green, for wood. The Shang made metal (bronze), white. The Zhou chose red for fire. In this cycle the next color was black, water. Taking black as his color was good politics!

Han Dynasty

Expanding China

How does a Chinese peasant with a dragon forehead and 72 black moles get to rule most of East Asia? How does he get farmers to become pioneers? How does he get horse-herding tribesmen thousands of miles from his capital city to say he is their emperor?

First he leads a rebellion against the Qin dynasty. The second Emperor of the Qin dynasty, Erhuangdi, had spent too much money on his tomb. He made the people pay high taxes and took them away from their farms to work without pay on government projects. Attacked by his own advisors, he escaped murder by committing suicide in his palace. Soon after, rebels burned his capital, Xianyang, to the ground. In 205 B.C., peasant leader Liu Bang, claimed the empire for himself. He began the Han dynasty.

The new emperor chose the people for his government not because they were princes but because they could do their jobs. Bright-but-ordinary men had the opportunity to work hard and get ahead. The government included scientists and engineers who studied, built, and invented for the empire. This was the Confucian way.

Protected by the peace of the Han dynasty, and connected by new roads, farmers moved to the frontier. Workers wove silk, made cast iron, drilled for salt and gas, and grew grain. Nomads along the frontier wanted these products. The Chinese used their wealth and technology to tempt nomads into the empire or to pay the armies sent to fight them. Han China grew to include most of East Asia.

MAKING SALT

Salt can be made in different ways. People let sea water evaporate in the sun or salt can be mined from the ground. In Han China, they also made it from salty water pumped out of the ground. They boiled the water until only salt remained. The tricky part was to get the water from hundreds or thousands of feet underground.

They built bamboo towers that looked like modern oil derricks. Each tower had a platform. An iron bit hung from a special bamboo cable that went from the platform to the ground. The cable was attached to a lever on a platform. Two or more men took turns jumping on and off the lever to make the bit go up and down. Another man centered the bit over the hole it was digging in the ground.

Workers could drill three feet in a day. If they drilled long enough, they hit brine water. Many wells were 3,000 feet deep and one was 4,800 feet deep—almost a mile! They pumped the brine water to the surface and boiled it to make salt.

竹木下

Iron, Salt, and Gas

Drilling for Profit

The sun is setting. Workers are coming home from a long, cold, winter day. One man moves from light to light, starting the gas lights for the evening. The street warms in their glow. Mothers smile. It will be warm and light while they cook dinner tonight. This could be Victorian London or New York in the 1890s. Or it could be Han China in 100 B.C. How did some areas of China get gas lamps 2,000 years ago? The story starts with salt!

Salt was one of China's most valuable products. Salt may not seem like much, but in the ancient world there were no refrigerators. Salt not only made things taste good, it kept meat and vegetables from rotting. It helped regulate body chemistry. Chinese people needed salt, and foreign people traded for it.

Selling salt made so much money that Han emperors took over the salt and iron-making businesses to pay for expanding the empire. Later, they let people make salt for themselves, but they charged a high salt tax.

Because the Chinese knew how to cast iron, which can be made into very large pieces, they could make huge flat pans to boil the brine water. These pans sat in rows above the ground. Now they needed heat. Fortunately, with the brine water, they often found natural gas. Pure gas is explosive ... a hard lesson to learn!

They piped this gas through bamboo pipes into tanks and mixed it with air to keep it from exploding. Then they sent it into bamboo pipelines that ran under the cast iron boiling pans. Openings along the pipeline let gas escape. They lit it, making gas burners under their cast iron pans to boil the brine water until it evaporated and made salt.

Some villages near the salt works piped in natural gas for lighting or cooking. That's how the lights went on in 100 B.C.

21

Astronomy

Models of Heaven

ASTRONOMY AND ASTROLOGY

Astronomy and astrology are different. Astronomy is the science of the stars. Astrology uses that information to try to predict the future or to explain the past and present. Today we see a big difference between looking for facts about the universe and making predictions about luck, romance, and politics based on the stars. In ancient times, people didn't make that separation. They thought stars had powerful connections to our daily lives.

In ancient and medieval China, astrology was very important. Astrologers advised the emperor and probably helped to make important decisions. These educated men believed that changes in the stars could change people's lives.

LEGEND OF THE FIRST ASTRONOMERS

King Yao commanded 2 brothers, Xi and He, to watch the sun, the moon, and the stars. They were ordered to figure out the timing of the seasons for the people.

King Yao ordered Xi to go to the east to meet the sunrise and to watch over spring, and to go to the south to control summer. The king ordered He to go to the west to say good-bye to the setting sun and manage the fall, and to go north to supervise the winter. The brothers were the first government astronomers.

People didn't always know what the sky was. They looked at it, but they couldn't send space ships to explore it. Ancient people knew about the stars and the sun, but they didn't know how far away they were, or how they worked. They did know they could use their movements to keep track of seasons and time. They could also use the stars to tell directions at night.

Chinese emperors had astronomers study the sky and calculate their calendar. The calendar was especially important to show farmers when to plant and harvest. During the Han dynasty, astronomers held important positions in the emperor's court. One man, Zhang Heng, lived between A.D. 78 and 139. He was the Royal Astronomer. Zhang Heng understood the seasons and the movement of the sun. He knew about the equator and the poles of the earth. He built a model, called an armillary sphere, that showed the earth and the sky, the equator, the poles, and the horizon. He also built a seismograph to detect earthquakes, and made the first star map we know of that used straight lines for longitude. This map was like the later, European Mercator map.

Most of Zhang Heng's writings have been lost, but not before other scientists read and used them in their own work. We know about what Zhang Heng did from what other scientists wrote.

Ancient people didn't know what caused eclipses. They thought maybe the sun or the moon actually went away during an eclipse. Maybe something ate them, and then vomited them back! Maybe they both gave out light and for some reason, the light faded and then came back on. Or maybe the eclipse was caused by shadows. We know the last idea was right.

What was the sky like? Was heaven an upside down bowl over the earth? Was it an egg shaped shell with the earth like the yolk at the center? Or was it empty space with the sun and the planets floating freely? Chinese astronomers had all these ideas. The one accepted around A.D. 300 was that the sky was like an egg and that the sun and stars orbited around the outside of it.

Modern astronomers still use the facts Chinese astronomers gathered about comets and eclipses. Their notes help today's scientists to track the paths of comets over hundreds of years.

COUNTING BEANS
Legend says King Yao kept an unusual calendar, a magic plant called the *mingjia*. The plant sprouted a bean every day for 15 days. Then one bean dropped off each day for 15 more. That way, the plant sprouted and dropped all its beans every 30 days. Chinese lunar months have either 29 or 30 days. In months with 29 days the last bean dried up on the plant.

ARMILLARY SPHERE
The armillary sphere measures the positions of stars, like a protractor for the sky, or a set of star rulers. The Chinese type has a circle for the equator, and one to show the paths of the sun, moon, and planets in the sky. It shows the poles. The pole of the sphere points to the north. The astronomer sights the star he wants to map through a tube. Measuring with the armillary sphere, he can find the the star's direction and distance from the North Pole.

Mandate from Heaven

Today leaders in many countries are elected. People follow them because they believe they were chosen the "right way." In China, the people believed in the emperor's "Mandate from Heaven." This meant the emperor ruled because he was good. His goodness would be reflected throughout the universe. People believed the heavens, the earth, the dead, and the living were one unit . . . like an orchestra, with many instruments.

If the emperor ruled his people in harmony, it was the will of the universe for him to continue to rule. If he was a bad ruler, other parts of the universe would go bad too. Floods or earthquakes might destroy whole regions. Comets could appear in the sky. People would suffer and his "mandate" to rule, his authority, would be taken away by heaven itself.

In order to keep his "Mandate from Heaven," an emperor had to explain the natural events that happened while he ruled. He could not stop comets or eclipses, but if he could predict them, people accepted them as part of an orderly plan.

When floods, earthquakes, or comets surprised people, they thought the emperor CAUSED the disasters by being a bad ruler. Helping people after earthquakes or floods wasn't just important because the victims needed help. Unhappy peasants, thinking the emperor had done something bad, could rebel. If he sent quick relief, or prevented disaster, he might also stop plots of revolution.

A Chinese emperor needed astronomers, mathematicians, engineers, and clear thinkers to help him keep order in the empire.

Seismograph

Taking the Pulse of an Empire

Zhang Heng designed the first seismograph to record earthquakes. His seismograph couldn't measure the size of a quake the way modern ones do, but it could alert officials to small or faraway quakes that they couldn't feel. He had the machine cast in bronze. In the middle was a column that vibrated during an earthquake. When the column vibrated it caused one of the eight dragon heads on the outside of the machine to drop a ball into the mouth of a bronze frog that sat below. The ball landed with a loud clang! That was the earthquake alarm. Where was the quake? The dragon that dropped the ball usually pointed to the earthquake. Scientists had to investigate to find exactly where the quake happened.

The outside of Zhang Heng's seismograph had eight dragons ready to drop eight balls into the mouths of eight frogs.

The inside might have had a thin column with a heavy ball weight at the top. This would move with movements of the earth.

At the top of the machine were two rings with eight tracks cut in them each leading to a dragon's mouth. Sandwiched between the rings were "sliders," or small metal pieces, that moved down a track if the pin on the ball weight touched them. The sliders knocked the ball out of one dragon's mouth.

Chances were, when an earthquake happened, the pin would move into one slot, push the slider, and continue to shake. Because of the shaking, it wouldn't be able to return to the center of the rings and go in another slot. Only one dragon dropped its ball.

Silk Road

Trading Ideas

Ancient Chinese used lengths of silk like money. During the Han Dynasty, soldiers on the frontier were paid with silk, and the government kept warehouses of silk at its outposts on the edges of the empire. From there, the empire sent gifts of silk to nomad tribes to buy their loyalty. The rest of the world wanted Chinese silk too!

A Roman author, Pliny the Elder, complained that the Roman Empire was wasting its money, sending it all to China to buy silk! Even in ancient times, traders carried Chinese silk to western Asia and Rome. The trade was booming.

The road across Asia to the Mediterranean got its name from all that silk ... the Silk Road. From Changan, capital of the Qin, Han, and Tang dynasties, it led across the Asian deserts and mountains to the Middle East and into Southern Europe.

The Silk Road wasn't just a road, it was an event. Traders didn't have trucks or trains. They carried Chinese silk, bronze, lacquerware, and jade in wagons or on camels across 5,000 or more miles . . . almost quarter of the way around the world! The road was long and hard. It was hot or cold, often steep and often empty. Oasis towns and trading centers dotted the route. The same caravan might not carry cargo all the way from Changan to Rome. A bolt of silk might be traded several times as it crossed Asia. But it got to Rome, probably on the back of a cud-chewing camel!

On the return trip, the caravans loaded up with Roman glass, amber, wool, linen, and coral. They brought animals . . . elephants, lions, and birds . . . and slaves back to China. Central Asia sent China raisins, wine, furs, and horses.

Traders in Central Asia made a good living buying and selling Chinese products. To protect their business, these traders tried to keep the Chinese from dealing directly with buyers in the Roman Empire and, later, in Medieval Europe. Columbus and other European explorers were searching for a way around the Silk Road. They were looking for a direct route to the Chinese things they wanted so much.

Along with trade came ideas. Travelers on the Silk Road carried information about the places they had visited. It is possible ideas about astronomy, mathematics, and papermaking traveled this road with the caravans.

Foreigners on the Silk Road

Making Silk

Who would imagine worms (silk moth larvae) could make cloth? Someone in China did. The Chinese were the first silk makers. We know in Shang and Zhou times they planted mulberry trees to feed the silkworms and built special rooms for the worms to spin their cocoons. Women raised the silk worms. Silk thread brought extra money to the farm.

The government collected taxes in lengths of cloth. Emperors used silk to coax nomadic tribes into the empire. Desire for silk brought foreigners to China. Silk was valuable and still is.

1

2

(1) Silkworms mate and lay their eggs on paper. The egg papers are hung inside over the winter. In the spring, silkworms hatch and women put them in a silk-worm room to feed on mulberry leaves. Adult silkworms are put on bamboo screens to spin their cocoons. Finally, the cocoons are steamed to kill the worms and to soften the silk.

(2) A worker finds the ends of the silk fibers in the water, winds the silk off the cocoon and wraps it onto a spool for spinning. Then silk threads are woven into cloth.

Tang Dynasty
International Attitude

The Tang capital, Changan, became the center of an international community. Caravans traveled back and forth along the Silk Road and south into India. People from all over Asia came to Changan to learn Chinese ideas, and the Chinese accepted them. Between 600 and 900, Changan was one of the most wonderful cities in the world.

During this time, printing began. Buddhists, anxious to spread their teachings, made some of the first printed pages. They made Buddha figures in stone, metal, and on paper to show their faith. The more the better. Printing was a fast, easy way to make many Buddhas. Later, people began to print calendars, charms, and religious books. Foreigners were welcomed into Changan, the capital, and brought their foods, music, and ideas with them. The Tang dynasty had an attitude ... new ideas were all right. Printing made it easier to spread them, and no government officials tried to stop it.

Printing would become common and artistic during the next dynasty, the Song. But its beginnings were in the Tang, when many nations and religions met in China.

Despite the best predictions and potions, no dynasty lasts forever. The Han dynasty was followed by 300 years of fighting for control. Nomad tribes invaded parts of North China, where they set up their own dynasties. Many Chinese moved south, taking their ideas and their agriculture with them. Buddhists from India arrived in China. The Buddhist religion began to spread. People liked the Buddhist ideas of heaven filled with palaces and trees that dripped jewels. They liked the Buddhist teaching of kindness and helping others. Some rulers became Buddhists. Chinese people, tired of war and change, were eager for the comfort of a new religion and new ideas. More and more of them became Buddhists too.

In 581, Yang Jian reunited China. He became Emperor Sui Wendi. He and his son sent farmers to build roads, canals, and new capitals. They repaired the Great Wall, then sent out their armies to conquer the North. They demanded too much from the people. After just 23 years, a civil war broke out. Army commanders joined bandits and overworked government laborers to fight the Sui. In 617, a Sui commander, Li Yuan, won the capital and started a new dynasty, the Tang.

Tang rulers were from the Northwest and had married into some nomad tribes. Tang leaders traced their ancestors to Lao Zi. They favored Daoism but allowed Buddhism, Islam, and other religions to prosper.

The Buddhist text, *Diamond Sutra,* was printed in 868.

Printing

Spreading the Word

Chinese people were used to making copies with backwards words. They stamped coins, pressed official seals, and carved bronze molds backwards. That may be why they invented block printing around 710. Before that, people copied books by hand. Sometimes they carved important messages in stone so they would last a long time. People learned to put paper over the stone messages and rub the paper with ink to copy the whole page. Almost like a block print! A block print is a full page carved into wood like the words on a rubber stamp. Printers can use that wooden page to made hundreds of copies.

To make a block print, a calligrapher, or an expert in beautiful writing, copied pages onto thin paper. The printer glued the paper, face down, onto a block of wood. The characters showed through the paper, like a tracing. They were backwards.

Trained carvers cut away the wood between the characters. Now the wood block had raised backwards characters like the reversed words on a rubber stamp.

The printer spread ink on the block, laid a paper across it, and rubbed the ink into the paper with a special pad. Then he hung up the paper to dry.

One book might need hundreds of wood blocks, but the printer could store the blocks to use again.

MOVEABLE TYPE

Moveable type lets a printer set lines of single characters in a frame, print the page, and then remove the characters to use in another page. Bi Sheng, a Chinese printer, made the first set of moveable type around 1041. He made his characters out of baked clay, glued them into a special iron frame with wax and pine sap, and then used the frame to print his pages. When he was done, he melted the wax, and put away the characters until he needed them again. When he died, he willed this prized possession to the nephews of writer Shen Kuo.

Even after Bi Sheng invented moveable type, block printing stayed popular in China. Why? The Chinese language is written with characters. Each word is shown with a different character or set of characters. Chinese used so many characters that a medieval printer might need hundreds of thousands of pieces of type.

A printer turns the wheel to find the right piece of moveable type.

Monkey King

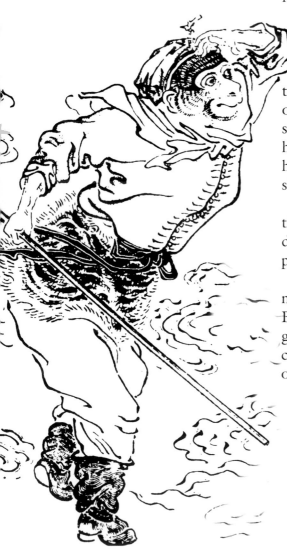

Monkey King could change into anything he liked . . . a bug, a tiger, a hundred-thousand-foot monkey. He carried a magic club which he disguised as a needle behind his ear. He could ride the clouds faster than any Chinese god, flying from continent to continent in a breath. Sound like a super hero? Monkey King is the star of a novel written in the 1500s by Wu Chengen. Monkey's tricks and high spirits made him so popular that he became a folk hero like King Arthur or Paul Bunyan.

His story tells how he became King of the Monkeys, learned his powers, and demanded a place in heaven. There the Jade Emperor made him a stable boy. But Monkey was full of tricks and made a mess of heaven. It took the Jade Emperor, all his army, and Buddha himself to catch Monkey and put him in a mountain for 500 years.

Released by a Buddhist holy woman, Monkey overcame his fun-loving, troublemaking self and used his powers to protect a saintly monk. The monk was traveling from China to India in order to carry back the Buddhist scriptures, the Tripitaka. These would give the Chinese instructions for living well and getting eternal life.

Monkey and his friends Pigsy, Sandy, and a magic dragon-horse, traveled with the monk across Asia for 14 years. They fought armies of ghosts and demons, crossed flaming mountains, and tricked monsters. When one demon's wife refused to help them, Monkey turned himself into a tiny bug and flew into her stomach. There he turned himself into a mini-monkey and kicked and pounded her insides until she agreed to help.

In the end, Monkey and the pilgrims arrived in the West, received the scriptures and were magically carried back to China in just eight days. The Chinese emperor ordered copies made of the scriptures to protect the precious originals.

Although there really wasn't a Monkey King, there was a Buddhist monk, Xuan Zhuang, who DID travel to India and return with many Buddhist texts. He spent years translating them from the Indian language, Sanskrit, to Chinese. The Tang emperor had the translations copied and sent throughout the empire. These copies are some of the oldest printing ever found.

Changing Dynasties

Dynasties are governments led by a powerful family. The Chinese Emperor was called the "Son of Heaven." His government was considered heavenly. But dynasties came and went. Why didn't they last forever? In China, when the emperor died his son or another family member (including one Tang empress) became emperor. People close to the emperor could try to change who the next emperor would be. The empress might have a favorite son in mind. An official, longing for personal power, could plot to choose a weak or stupid relative. Sometimes people killed the emperor . . . to replace him. The emperor got his power not only from his God-like position, but also from his family and officials. They could do him in.

The emperor was supported by officials, landlords, and military men. His decisions changed their lives. He could change their job or where they lived, or he might give favors to other people and not to them. These middle officials knew many people. They could organize peasants for or against the government. The emperor needed their loyalty.

Most Chinese people were peasants. Every year they paid taxes in grain and cloth. They had to spend part of the year working for free on government projects like digging the Grand Canal or building 40-to-50-foot high city walls. They could be called away to fight wars. When the emperor asked for a lot, the peasants paid. When the emperor wanted less, the peasants' lives were easier.

Emperors changed because of death or palace plots. Dynasties changed when angry peasants revolted, or when the army was too weak to protect China from invaders. At the end of a dynasty, there were usually years of war to see who would have the power to build a new dynasty. Men who started new dynasties were strong soldiers and strong leaders. They had to win many battles and get the support of the educated people before they could claim the emperor's throne.

Time in Chinese history is measured by dynasties. This is an easy way to divide thousands of years. Dynasties could last just a few years or as long as three or four hundred years.

WEN AND WU

In Chinese tradition, society depended on a mix of strength, wu, and thought, wen. Strength kept enemies away and punished criminals. Strength kept order. But the Chinese believed the more important ingredient was thought . . . culture. Culture made the Chinese people special. Culture was what the outside world wanted. Through study, art, and literature, the Chinese bettered themselves. Wen and wu needed to be balanced, but wen (thought) was better. Knowledge is power.

Song Dynasty
Ideas and Inventions

As more Chinese moved to southern China, there wasn't enough rice for all of them. The Emperor learned of a kind of rice that grew more grain on each plant. In 1012, he ordered 30,000 bushels of the new rice seed imported from Champa, near today's Vietnam. Then he ordered officials to teach farmers to plant it. Farmers could plant the new rice twice each year, making twice as much rice and twice as much work. Now there was plenty of food. Changing to the new rice helped feed China for the next centuries. Learning and power combined to help China.

A young man could help himself and his family by studying for civil service exams. A government position was a good job. In a country divided into upper-class and ordinary people, studying was a way to get ahead.

What would happen if instead of having a coach, a football team had 11 players who wanted to call the plays? Do you think they'd end up fighting? The Tang dynasty ended when the emperor's "team" of military governors, who were supposed to protect China's borders, decided they wanted more power. The emperor couldn't control them. Nomads attacked and governors and generals fought each other. China was crisscrossed with wars. Armies destroyed farms. Villagers were sent to war. Princes were murdered. Between 907 and 960 northern China had five dynasties.

In 960 a military commander, Zhao Kuangyin, won the empire. He began the Northern Song dynasty. He didn't control all of China. Nomad nations, Turks and Mongols, held much of China's land. The Song dynasty was one of many competing countries in East Asia. In fact, if there had been T.V. or newspapers in 900–1200, North China might have been called a political "hot spot." Starting a Chinese dynasty didn't settle the disagreements in East Asia.

But the emperor could control the generals and powerful families. Song emperors replaced military commanders with civilian officials. They believed Confucius' teachings of order and responsibility. When the Song government needed officials it didn't go to powerful families or the military. It expanded a system where students took tests to get government jobs. The best students, not some important man's son, got jobs. This civil service system, the model for many used today, was the first in the world.

The examination students needed material to study. New government officials needed information. The Song government started large print shops to copy the writings of Confucius and government documents. For the first time, there were many books.

During the Song dynasty, there was information, order, and respect for learning. There was an "explosion" of great art, great literature, and new inventions. Engineers built locks on canals to raise and lower boats without losing their loads. The Chinese invented the spinning wheel, modernizing silk making. They attached gun powder to crossbow arrows and made bombs. Mathematicians used the abacus, a kind of hand powered calculator.

It was in this time that Su Song invented the first mechanical clock.

Su Song's Clock

Perfect Timing

Su Song, born in 1020, was a respected government official . . . honest and a gentleman. He was an advisor to the emperor. The emperor sent Su Song on a special trip to see the emperor of Liao, the country to the north. Su Song was to greet the Liao emperor on his birthday. This ceremony would help keep peace between the two countries.

Su Song arrived a day early. Embarrassed, he realized that the astronomers in China had made a mistake. The emperor's birthday was the next day. He apologized, saying that great empires had different calendars and both must be respected. The Liao emperor agreed. But when he returned to Kaifeng, Su Song and the Song Emperor were both upset. The Chinese should have a correct clock and calendar, like the Liao.

Su Song suggested designing a new clock. The emperor agreed and gave him a team of at least 12 men to work on the project. One, Han Gonglian, was a fine mathematician. He designed the clock.

The clock took 8 years to build. It was 30 feet high. The outside was a 5-story tower. Little carved people appeared in its windows clanging bells and pounding drums to show the hours. (Chinese measured time in double hours. There were 12 Chinese hours in a day.) On top of the clock was a huge, armillary sphere. It turned with the hours, showing the position of the stars at the time. The whole clock was powered by water.

Su Song was an old man when the clock was finished. After he died, the Jin (a nomad group) invaded Kaifeng. The emperor escaped to the south leaving the huge clock behind. The conquerors took the clock apart and carried the pieces in carts and wagons to their capital in the north. They put up the clock, but they didn't take care of it. Within a few years it was broken. Only the armillary sphere was left. In 1215, Mongols invaded the city where it stood. When the Jin ran away, the sphere was left behind again. No one knows what happened to it.

Water had always been used to make clocks work. In the older clocks, water dripped out of a bowl at a set speed. The water level told the time. In Su Song's clock, the falling water turned a water wheel with a drive shaft over 20 feet long that turned the clockworks. The movements of the water, gears, and shafts had to be figured mathematically to work together perfectly.

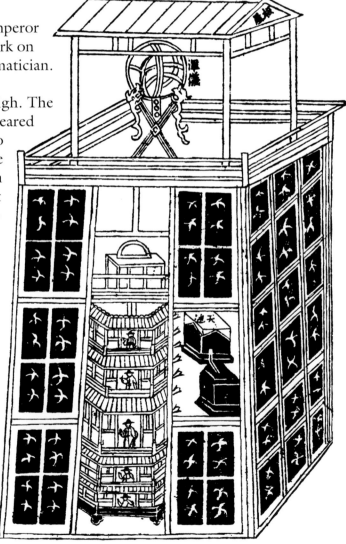

MAGIC SQUARES
In ancient China numbers were used in government and religious rituals. These magic squares have their own story!

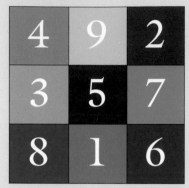

What is the magic in this magic square? Add the 3 numbers in each row across or each column up and down. What number do you get? Now add the 3 numbers in the diagonal lines. Do you get the same number? Legend says this magic square was a gift from a Turtle in the Lo River to the Emperor Yu.

Counting in Chinese

Chinese numbers are different from the Arabic numbers we use. They are:

	Say	Write			Write	Say
1	yi	一	20	(two ten)	二十	er shi
2	er	二	30	(three ten)	三十	san shi
3	san	三	40	(four ten)	四十	si shi
4	si	四	50	(five ten)	五十	wu shi
5	wu	五	60	(six ten)	六十	liu shi
6	liu	六	70	(seven ten)	七十	qi shi
7	qi	七	80	(eight ten)	八十	ba shi
8	ba	八	90	(nine ten)	九十	jiao shi
9	jiao	九				
10	shi	十				
0	ling	零				
			100		一百	bai

Now you can write numbers up to 100:

26 is er shi (20) liu (6)   二十六
42 is si shi (forty) er (two)   四十二
99 is jiao shi jiao.   九十九

Today, you will see Chinese numbers in signs, in books, and newspapers. When Chinese people do their math, they use Arabic numbers . . . the same ones you use.

This square was a gift from the Dragon Horse of the Yellow River. Take an outside number from the puzzle. Subtract the number next to it. What is your answer? Try another pair. Do you get the same number? Add the odd numbers (but not the 5). Add the even numbers. What number do you get?

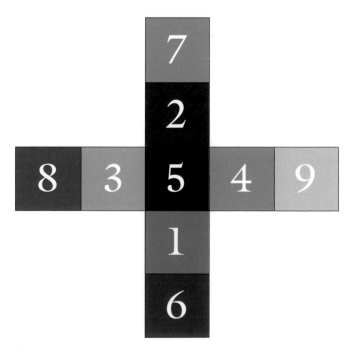

Counting Rods and the Abacus

Seeing Value

The first Chinese math was done with counting rods. The idea was simple. Rods showed numbers.

1 to 5 were made like this: ▬ ═ ☰ ☰ ☰

Then rods were added from 6 to 9 like this: ⊥ ⊥ ⊥ ⊥

Counting rods were laid out in 2 different ways. Numbers in the 1s, 100s, 10,000s columns were laid up and down. Numbers in the 10s, 1,000s, 100,000s columns were laid across. This way it was clear where one set of rods ended and the next began.

This number is 123: | ═ |||

At first, the Chinese left a space when they meant 0. They added 0 later. Counting rods had place value like our decimal system . . . 1s, 10s, 100s, etc. Chinese counting rods were the first decimal system.

Although the math worked, using counting rods was clumsy. Harder math needed something easier to use. The abacus was the answer. The abacus, which may or may not have been invented in China, replaced counting rods with beads strung on wires. The first 4 rods are the same as the first 4 beads. The 5 rod is like the top bead of the abacus, above the bar. Each line of beads is like one of our columns . . . 1s, 10s, 100s, 1,000s.

If you know how to use an abacus you can add, subtract, multiply, and divide very quickly. It is easier than it looks!

While most folks used math to keep track of important things like pigs or money owed for rice, government mathematicians calculated the positions of stars, made accurate calendars, or plotted maps. Scholars looked for perfect relationships between numbers, and for mathematical patterns in music. They searched for harmony and balance in the universe through numbers.

Chinese mathematicians helped to develop algebra. Arab, Indian, and Chinese thinkers all contributed to algebra. The ideas were passed back and forth through Asia, getting more powerful as different people added new thoughts.

Han dynasty people carried 271 counting rods in a handy bag! A law said Tang officials had to carry counting rods with them just in case they needed to do some math. By the Song and Yuan dynasties some people were using the abacus. The abacus became a household item later, during the Ming dynasty, and is still used today.

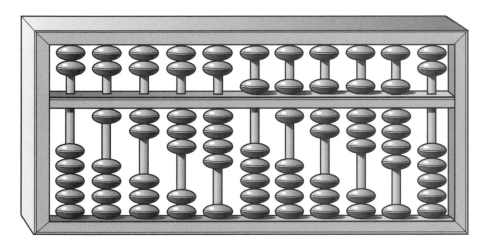

The Chinese abacus has 5 beads below the bar that stand for one unit each and 2 beads above the bar that stand for 5 units each. The second five bead is used for division problems. This number is 1,234,567,890.

Mongols
Invaders from the North

The Mongols were not well educated. They brought foreigners from Central Asia and even Europe to help run their government. Marco Polo served in Kublai Khan's court. Most Chinese officials weren't allowed to work in the Mongol government. They were free to study privately, adding to the culture that grew so well during the Song.

When the Mongol leader, Khublai Khan, built his capital at Beijing, or when Mongol ships sailed against Japan, the compasses they used were Chinese. Although the northerners had won the Chinese land, every compass pointed south. That's the Chinese way.

After Kaifeng (and Su Song's clock) was captured by invaders, times changed in China. The Song leaders fled to the south. North China was ruled by nomad groups: the Qidan (Liao), the Tanguts (Xixia), the Ruzhens (Jurchens) (Jin), and the Mongols. The Mongols, led by Genghis Khan, had plans to conquer the world. They were born riders who attacked on horseback. When the Mongols captured a town they often enlisted the town's men in their army (threatening to kill those who didn't join). Then they pushed on to take over the next town. Mongol horsemen conquered Central Asia, Persia, and Russia. They attacked as far west as Poland and Hungary and to the south they captured Bagdad. Then they turned their attention to China.

The Song dynasty had regrouped in south China and continued to be Chinese. There, it trained students to work for the government. It organized craftsmen to make steel and porcelain. As more Chinese fled the north to southern China, it was hard to grow enough rice for everyone. The government ordered farmers to plant new kinds of rice from Southeast Asia. Then there was plenty. The Chinese traded silks for spices in India. Chinese scholars wrote and thought about old ways and their new government. Artists and calligraphers painted. While the nomads to the north fought for power, Song China was becoming very "Chinese."

But the government tried to buy off, and then to support the wrong nomads. Although Song troops helped the Mongols defeat the Jin, the Song became the Mongols' next target. They could hold off, but they couldn't stop the Mongols. In 1279, 40 years after their first attack on Song China, the Mongols had conquered all of China. They called their dynasty the Yuan.

Compass

Direction of Fortune

Chinese legend says the Yellow Emperor, God of the Universe, lived in the center of the world, and four other gods ruled the north, south, east, and west. From the earliest times, Chinese people believed directions were powerful. The Shang people built walled cities where most doors and graves faced south. Directions were so important in ceremonies, in religion, and in daily life that the Chinese found a way to measure them. They invented the compass.

These compasses were different. The needles on our compasses point north. The line of the needle, in fact, points north AND south. In China, south was the most important direction. Their compasses pointed south! And the first ones (from about 100) didn't have needles. Instead they had a magnetic stone shaped like a fish or spoon that turned to show the direction. The first compass that we know had a needle was made in 570.

How did they use these first compasses? Not to find directions in the night or to plot courses across oceans. They were used to find the best places for buildings and graves. The Chinese believed that certain placements were lucky and good and others could bring misfortune. Men called geomancers used complicated compasses to find the right spots. The rules and ideas they used are called feng shui. Feng shui is still used today.

Compasses used for guiding Chinese ships are first mentioned around 1090. Zhu Yu, from Guangdong, said Chinese ship pilots used south-pointing needles to steer in bad weather. The Korean, Ch'oe Pu, wrote in his diary that his ship's captain used a south-pointing needle to direct their ship before it was pushed off course by a powerful storm.

Many feng shui beliefs are practical: face a building south for warmth and light, build near water. Some are more like interior design. Stairs running to the front door will let good qi escape. Long lines of doors and windows should be broken up with a windchime or curtain. The way a person faces when sleeping can improve his fortune. The idea is to keep the good qi in and the bad qi out.

Animal Guardians of the Four Directions

Black Tortoise (Black Warrior) of the north

Azure Dragon of the east

White Tiger of the west

Red Bird of the south

These animals are written about in legends and are often found carved or painted in tombs.

Qi

Invisible Power

Many people have stories of seeing water dowsers find water with a forked stick. How do they do that? Is it magic? We know they do find water. There are old wives tales that don't make sense but are true. New fences built during a full moon will warp, joints ache when it's going to rain. People everywhere have practical folk beliefs.

In China, some people have a special group of beliefs, feng shui. Imagine the sky, the wind, the stars in the sky. Imagine the water on the ground and under the ground. In ancient China this wind and water . . . feng shui . . . described the environment. These folk beliefs are an ancient environmental movement. Over centuries, studying the environment and its effect on humans has become a specialty of certain people. They are feng shui men or geomancers.

They can use their knowledge to decide where to place buildings or graves so the people who use them, whether living or dead, will be happy and lucky. They believe the earth and everything living has an energy force called qi. Think of qi as invisible energy, like radio waves, that we can't explain yet. Qi means air. Qi gives life. It moves over the earth, around trees, even through our bodies. Qi travels best in straight lines. There is good qi and bad qi.

Qi travels through the earth and on it. Rivers, lakes, and hills all form the body of the earth. If people decide to cut the earth to make a building or a grave, it must be done carefully, to do the least damage. Bad cuts can release bad qi, or they can cause the earth to suffer. Feng shui experts must choose a good place to build.

The direction that a building faces is important. Each direction has a meaning. Doors facing south are usually more lucky than doors facing north. A special compass is used to decide which direction a building will face.

Today, some people believe in feng shui and some don't. In Hong Kong or in San Francisco's Chinatown a feng shui expert may be asked to help decide the arrangement of a business office or the architecture of a new building. This may seem superstitious, but even people who don't believe in feng shui say that they've seen it work. One man changed the angle of his desk and his luck changed. Is this because he already believed he would have good luck? No one can say.

Cultivating Our Bodies

Chinese medicine is about staying healthy. To think like a traditional Chinese doctor, begin by thinking like a gardener. Say you want to grow a pumpkin for the county fair. You plant the seed carefully, protect it from birds and insects, water it and weed around it. You keep it warm when it's sprouting and feed it as it grows. The plant needs constant care.

Traditional Chinese medicine sees the body like a garden . . . not surprising since most Chinese people were and still are farmers. Our bodies must have the right foods and exercises. They shouldn't get too hot or too cold. We shouldn't eat too much food, or too little food. Too much of anything . . . sleep, exercise, spicy foods, is not good. The person, or the doctor, watches the body constantly and makes changes when they are needed.

Traditional doctors think about balance (yin and yang) and energy (qi) in our bodies. All things are best when the yin and yang are balanced. In medicine, yin is cold and inside, yang is warm and outside. If we have a fever, that is yang. The chills would be yin. They need to be balanced.

Qi is the natural energy that moves through our body. Qi should flow freely, like water through a stream. If it is stopped or weakened we feel bad. Doctors use acupuncture to release or move qi. Some people learn to move qi in special ways through their bodies. This takes practice. People who study tai ji (taijiquan) learn to direct their own qi.

Chinese Medicine

Practice Makes Perfect

If you fall off your bike and break your arm you can call the doctor or go to the emergency room. If you are in a car accident, someone may call 911. The Shang people didn't have telephones or modern hospitals but they did have doctors. Archeologists have found notes about diseases and toothaches written on Shang tortoise shells and bones.

Early Chinese doctors collected information about the human body, healing plants, and diseases. They passed their knowledge down to younger doctors, often sons. They wrote books. *The Canon of Medicine,* written around 300 B.C., lists 311 diseases including diabetes, asthma, tumors, and mumps. It teaches about acupuncture, moxibustion, oral drugs, and surgery.

Another book from the same time gives prescriptions for curing diseases and tells how to examine a patient. It even tells how to save a hanging victim with CPR (they didn't call it that). Since then, Chinese traditional doctors have written at least 8,000 books on medicine.

How did the first doctors learn what to do? Probably through trial and error. They tried different herbs and healing mixtures, then wrote down or memorized what happened. Chinese doctors probably helped wounded soldiers. Maybe they learned about surgery, pain control, and the way the body worked by helping the battle victims. Modern scientists have proven what doctors knew then . . . their medicine worked.

Chinese doctors treated their patients with stone needles called *bian* during the Stone Age. They placed needles at special points on the body to stop pain, or to help healing. Stone needles were replaced by metal ones around 800 B.C. This was the beginning of acupuncture. Acupuncture is still used today for everything from headaches to hepatitis to putting people to sleep before surgery. The doctor places needles at points along invisible lines (meridians) to correct the flow of qi and heal the body. The points where she uses needles aren't always near the places they help. A point on the foot, for example, can help the liver. The needles look a little scary, but they don't hurt much. The patient feels energy near the needle. It usually feels good, although sometimes it can be intense. Traditional doctors usually use finger pressure instead of acupuncture needles on children.

Another treatment is moxibustion. The doctor burns the herb mugwort above special places on the patient's body. Moxibustion, like acupuncture, stimulates exact body points with heat. Although acupuncture and moxibustion may seem odd to some people, they

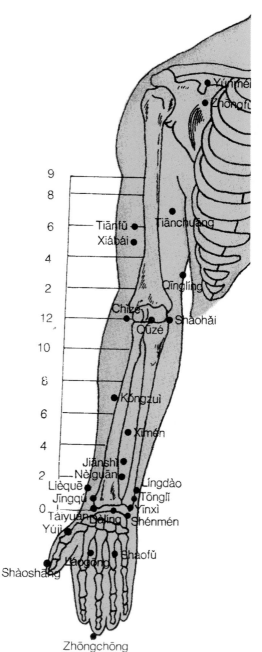

work. And to millions of Chinese and Asian people they are not odd at all. They are practical treatments their doctors use.

Today, the government of the People's Republic of China is training more traditional doctors. Traditional medicine is not expensive. It doesn't need a lot of special equipment. Traditional doctors can help people in the cities and in the farthest corners of China. Chinese medicine is also used in Japan, Southeast Asia, Korea, and throughout the world. Chinese people living in other countries often prefer to go to traditional doctors. Anyone can see a Chinese traditional doctor and many people, from all backgrounds, do.

When a traditional Chinese doctor says, "Say ah," she's not just looking for a red throat. She wants to see your tongue! The doctor gets information from looking at the color and condition of the tongue.

When you visit a traditional doctor, he or she will ask about your health. He'll talk to you about how you are feeling, about family, school, or job. He knows what is happening around you can change your health. He'll ask about what you eat and how you are sleeping. Then he will take your pulse.

He doesn't count pulse rate the way a nurse in a hospital does. He takes your pulse with three fingers, pushing lightly, then medium and then firmly on your wrist. The traditional doctor feels 28 different pulses. Each one tells him about a different body system.

Next he looks at your tongue. Is it red or fuzzy? Pink and smooth? He uses all this information to decide how to treat you. He may give you advice about eating or exercising, tell you not to eat some foods, or to drink some tea. He may tell you not to work so hard or to settle an argument with a friend! Or he may treat you with herbs mixed from special recipes, or with acupuncture, acupressure, or moxibustion. Traditional treatment may take many visits to the doctor. Because it is natural, it works more gradually than Western medicine does.

THE DIVINE PEASANT
Chinese medicine is so old there is a legend to explain it. The Emperor of the South, who was the god of the sun, taught people how to grow grain. People called him the Divine Peasant. He was also the god of medicine. He created poisonous plants and plants that cure diseases. He tested these on himself, sometimes poisoning himself and getting well as many as 70 times in a day.

41

Ming Dynasty
Marketing China

You may be used to eating on plastic, or paper plates. Maybe you eat a burger out of a bag. During the last couple of hundred years, people got so used to eating off porcelain plates that they named dishes for the country that invented porcelain . . . china! Porcelain is a special, delicate kind of pottery or baked clay. Pottery can be heavy and dark but porcelain, made from hard white clay, can be so thin you can see through it.

When you think of Chinese porcelain, you probably think of the blue and white dishes decorated with flowers, houses, dragons, or fish. You can buy dishes like that in any shop in the Chinese neighborhoods of San Francisco, Vancouver, or New York. This kind of porcelain became popular in the 1600s in Europe and Japan. It inspired European potters to try to learn to make it themselves. The Chinese weren't sharing their secrets. They used porcelain for trade.

Caravans carried Tang porcelain along the Silk Road. Archeologists have found Song dynasty porcelain in East Africa! During the Song and Yuan dynasties, the Chinese traded more and more with countries around the Indian Ocean.

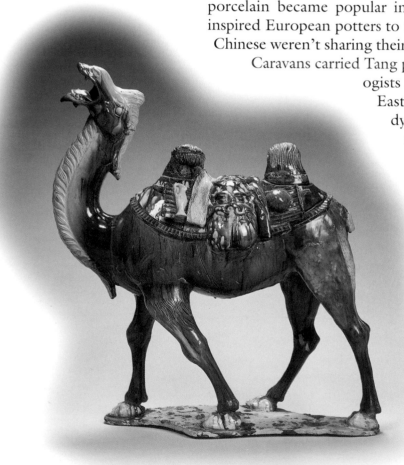

In 1368, Zhu Yuanzhang, a poor but tough peasant, led a rebel Chinese army to victory over the Yuan Mongols. He controlled China strictly under his new Ming dynasty. China was peaceful again. In the next 300 hundred years the population grew. People had more money to spend. Towns grew up around markets. Life was orderly and comfortable, especially in the south of China. The government, which still supported farming as the best job, frowned on buying and selling to make money. But there was money to be made. Many people chose to be traders. During the Ming dynasty, Chinese products were traded around the world. One of the favorites was porcelain.

Tang dynasty earthernware camel with 3–color glaze

Making Porcelain

Not all pottery is porcelain. Porcelain is made from special fine white clay. When it is fired (baked) at very high temperatures, chemicals change the clay. Fired porcelain is like a cross between glass and pottery. Yangshao people made the first Chinese pottery. The first porcelain, from the Han dynasty, wasn't as fine as porcelain that came later, like delicate green Song porcelain or blue and white or multi-colored pieces of the Ming and Qing dynasties. Today we can recognize porcelain from different dynasties and even from certain workshops.

For a long time only the Chinese knew how to make porcelain. Families passed their secrets on to sons. There were secrets about clay, firing temperatures, and mixing glazes (glass-like paint). The wrong heat would make a piece that was supposed to be green turn dark. The wrong amount of iron, copper, or cobalt in a glaze would change its color. Kiln (oven) fires had to be exactly the right temperature. In porcelain workshops, different workers became experts at the different jobs.

During the Song, the government set up workshops with huge kilns at Longquan (Dragon Spring). Called dragon kilns, they snaked up hillsides like dragons. The rising heat from fires at the bottom of the kilns gradually warmed the top section of the kilns. The most delicate pieces were fired in the top to protect them from fast temperature changes. Workers could load the Longquan kilns with 25,000 pieces at once.

Ming dynasty potters took 72 steps to change raw clay to porcelain. They pounded kaolin clay from Mt. Kaoliang and another clay called "porcelain stone" together for a whole day. (Kaolin is fine and white, porcelain stone contains feldspar, which creates the chemicals that make porcelain "glass-like.") Next, potters mixed the clay powder in water. The heaviest clay sank. They poured off the lighter clay (still mixed in the water) and let it dry into a super-fine powder.

They added enough water to the powder to make a thick paste, then pressed the clay into molds or shaped it into cups and plates on the potter's wheel. The shaped pieces needed to be dried, polished, and then decorated.

To make the famous blue and white porcelain, Ming potters painted designs on the dry pieces with cobalt before they were fired. They covered the pieces with a clear glaze and fired them for 24 hours!

Although people loved porcelain because it was beautiful, it had a more practical value. In China, mass produced porcelain was cheap enough for most families to own. The glazed plates were easier to keep clean (and germ free) than unglazed stoneware. Many people may have escaped disease and death by using porcelain.

Persians, Arabs, Egyptians, and Turks learned Chinese ways for making porcelain around 1000. Porcelain making came to Venice in 1470. Other Europeans were still trying to figure out how to make porcelain as late as the 1700s.

Arabs also learned to make paper from the Chinese. Europeans bought their paper from Arabs for several hundred years, until the Arabs set up paper mills in Spain.

Ming dynasty porcelain bowl (plate)

The Chinese used their thousand years of ship-building knowledge to outfit Zheng He's trips. He didn't travel light. On his first voyage he took 317 ships and 27,800 men. Sixty-two of the ships were huge treasure ships. These 440-foot ships were longer than a football field! They were probably six times longer than the largest ship Columbus would sail to the Americas 90 years later.

Zheng He

Sailing the Edge of the World

Do you like to give your friends gifts? Do you go to visit them? That's what friends do. And that's what the Chinese thought friends should do. When China took over new territory, or when Chinese officials met people in far-off lands, they invited them to visit the emperor. The emperor accepted their gifts and then he gave gifts to them. This was called tribute.

When the Ming dynasty began to control new territory, governments from around Asia sent officials to Beijing to honor the emperor. The emperor prized these friendships. To him, they showed that other countries accepted China as their most powerful neighbor.

Between 1405 and 1433, the Ming emperor sent his minister Zheng He, on seven different voyages around the Indian Ocean. Zheng He, a Moslem, was chosen to chase a fleeing Mongol emperor to the Moslem lands in the West. He didn't find his man, but he carried the emperor's good wishes to the governments there. He took gifts to far-off countries and brought back their tribute to China. Zheng He collected scientific information and brought home strange animals like giraffes.

Although Zheng He visited over 30 countries, he didn't try to take settlers or to trade. He was making friends for his government. Later on, the Ming government stopped the voyages. They were expensive and the government needed the money for wars. Some government officials were jealous of men like Zheng He. In 1479, one of them had all the records about Zheng He's journeys destroyed.

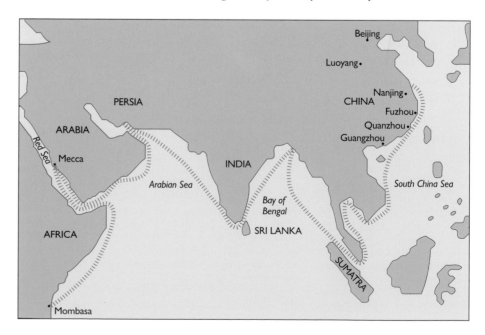

44

Building Better Ships

Before ships had motors, sailors staked their lives on the wind. A strong wind could rip sails or sink a ship. Without wind, ships floated for days at sea. The crew could run out of food or water. Winds blew ships off course, away from land, or to the wrong country. Sailing was dangerous. A good ship could deliver your cargo and save your life. The Chinese built good ships!

The Ming ships that Zheng He sailed followed almost 1500 years of Chinese pioneering in sailing. (Chinese inventors even put sails on wheelbarrows, using the wind to push the "sailing barrows.") Chinese ships, junks, became easier to steer and safer in storms with each invention shipmakers added. Improvements like moveable sails, rudders, and bulkheads are now used around the world.

Sea voyages were grand, but most Chinese ships sailed the canals that, by 1400, connected south China to Beijing. Canals made moving grain, cargo, and passengers easier.

Batten sails, (**A**) made of bamboo mats stretched between poles, can be lifted one piece at a time. Sailors can change each sail into a small sail or a big one. It's easy to stretch a batten sail tight to catch more wind. The sails are moveable. This lets sailors sail into the wind. The crew turns the sails so the boat moves across the water in a zigzag line (tacking).

Chinese boats were built with walls inside that divided them into spaces called bulkheads. Each space was sealed off from the other spaces. If a ship hit a rock or broke in a storm, water would only fill the space with the hole in it. Only one part would leak. Bulkheads made Chinese boats hard to sink.

A ship with a rudder (**B**) turns easier and faster than a ship without one. A rudder with holes in it turns a ship even faster. If you were sailing toward a rocky shore, you'd want a ship with a rudder!

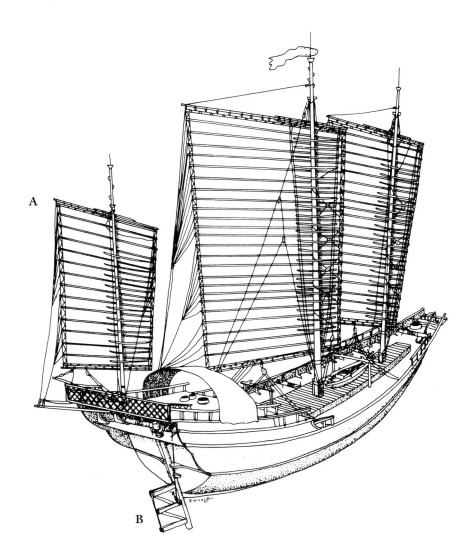

Changes

You hear a lot of talk about the world becoming smaller. We are in the jet age. There is an information highway out there. What we know, and what we are able to find out, is changing. During the 1500s, the world was changing too, for some of the same reasons. Ships were better. The world was getting "smaller." People who had known about each other only through stories and legends were about to meet. Europeans, longing to sail directly to China, made their voyages of discovery. They landed in the New World. People on all continents would feel the changes.

In China, there was enough to do just to keep the government going. China's population was growing. Tartars attacked North China. Japanese pirates raided the coast. To the northeast, the Manchus began to gain power. China hardly needed more "western barbarians" from Europe. The Chinese had a rich culture and all sorts of wonderful things. They believed in order, balance, and knowing what was enough. Change was not always good. The Chinese didn't see a reason to reach out to the rest of the world or to let the European barbarians (who did arrive by sea) in to trade.

But, in 1583, an Italian priest and scientist, Matteo Ricci, tempted the Chinese officials with his scientific knowledge. He was allowed into China to demonstrate European technology and astronomy. Oddly, he bribed several officials with European clocks so they would let him live in Beijing. (Remember, Su Song's grand clock had been lost for centuries.)

46

Ricci was accepted into the emperor's closest circle where he shared his Western knowledge with the Chinese. Chinese and Western science met. Ideas and inventions wouldn't be purely Chinese, or purely Western anymore. The "Chinese universe" changed forever.

European science began to change Chinese ideas. Chinese scholars wanted to learn about Western astronomy, geometry, and medicine. In the years that followed, the Chinese studied Western scientific methods. They used European weapons and European ideas of chemistry, physics, and engineering.

Chinese ideas and inventions had already been crossing continents for centuries. Travelers and emigrants, whether crossing the Silk Road or sailing the new, smaller world, carried with them ancient and practical knowledge. The ships Europeans sailed to Africa and the Americas used Chinese ideas for their sails, masts, and rudders. They navigated with the help of the compass, another Chinese invention. The moveable type used to print the books they carried to China and the gunpowder Europeans used on their warships were Chinese inventions.

Today, we see examples of Chinese inventions around the world . . . suspension bridges, canal locks, dike and levy systems on our rivers, oil derricks, the spinning wheel, even umbrellas. From kites to Chinese medicine, from fireworks to wheelbarrows, from spinning wheels to sailing ships, Chinese inventions changed our world.

Index

TA/140/01